I0428184

How To Understand And Stop Nuisance Direct Marketing Phone Calls, Texts & E-Mails In The UK

A Guide to Understanding Your Rights and How to Uphold Them.

By

Gillian King

CONTENTS

Introduction

This book is for people who are receiving advertising telephone calls, texts and emails they do not want. This type of contact is known as 'Direct Marketing' and can be extremely invasive in the lives of ordinary individuals. At best, it can be annoying; at worst, it can be very upsetting for people who live alone, particularly if it involves nuisance phone calls.

The aim of the book is to:

- Reassure people they are not alone with this problem.
- Explain what the law says about unwanted communications.
- Give an overview of the bodies that regulate the laws.
- Let people know what steps to take to try and minimise the problem.

How advertising tactics have changed

Ever since one person has had a product or service to sell to another, we have had advertising in some form. Many people from around age 40 upwards will remember the days when advertising was more generalised than it is today and happened from a reasonable distance, such as in a newspaper or magazine, on TV or radio and on billboards or posters informing us about anything from new cars to washing-up liquid.

While we may have thought advertising was 'in your face' back then, it was really nothing more than a whisper to our ears and eyes compared to the incessant and personalised 'poking' we all get now in many different forms.

With the boom in computers, mobile phones and other electronic gadgets came a new form of advertising which was much closer to home than billboard or magazine ads, in fact, it hit us right in the heart of our lives without us actively inviting it in. Our landline phones now ring constantly with someone selling something and our mobile phones ping with new messages every few minutes as marketing texts and emails come through.

The younger generation has grown up with this kind of marketing and has little or no experience of how advertising worked in the days before Information Technology made it easy to target us directly at home or on mobile devices.

The trend towards this direct and personal approach to advertising can feel threatening to people who grew up in a different era.

A more invasive approach to advertising

As more and more of our personal details are being stored on computers by websites where we buy goods and by big stores where we buy food, clothing and electrical items, it is getting more and more difficult, if not impossible to keep up with who is storing what information about us. People who buy online are constantly giving out valuable personal information and blindly hoping it is being processed and used appropriately.

There are many ways that businesses, from the trustworthy to the unscrupulous, can get hold of our personal contact information and even find out what our buying habits are.

We are no longer left alone to make up our own minds about when we need new windows, boilers, sofas or anything else we may want to buy. Nor are we left in peace to decide for ourselves, when it is time our sofa was replaced or where we might buy it. Instead, we are bombarded with advertising telling us we should buy a new this or that, not because the old thing might be worn out but because we are brainwashed into believing it is now 'unfashionable'.

Gone are the days when personal choice and free will were respected and given only a nudge by generalised advertising. We seem to have become, in the eyes of big business, sitting ducks in our own homes where our telephones and computers are used as more direct ways to tell us what we should be buying, when we should be buying it and from whom.

Even loud and incessant TV advertising pales into insignificance beside a personal phone call, direct to you, while you are eating your dinner, from a business that knows your name and wants your money but withholds its own number. You can turn a TV off or decide not to watch it at all but of course, it is not practical to leave phones and computers switched off to avoid being 'got at' by Direct Marketing.

There is a relentless assault on our minds and bank accounts as we move further and further away from being human beings to de-humanised piggy-banks for companies to keep shaking when it suits them.

I had one call where a young man selling solar panels told me, after ringing for the umpteenth time (without my consent), that he could call me whenever he wanted and there was nothing I could do about it.

This was after I told him I objected to his call. It was a very nasty, invasive call. I had already told him I did not want solar panels but he seemed to know better.

Our house just happens to be in the perfect position for collecting solar energy and we, along with several neighbours are plagued with approaches from solar panel companies who want to use our roofs to make money.

The argument I had with a total stranger, in the middle of dinner, was unpleasant and upsetting. It was as if he was trying to take possession of our roof against our will.

There is something badly wrong when people can call us up, ask us to spend money on something we clearly do not want and then turn nasty when we don't give them what they want. It is a bit like being mugged from a distance and grappling to hold onto our money, (or roof!) albeit over the phone.

In my experience, many of these types of calls are made in the early evening just when people are sitting down to relax and have dinner or watch TV.

Ending up in an argument with an arrogant sales person is the last thing anyone expects or wants.

Chapter 1 - How NOT to deal with unwanted sales calls.

For the last few years, I have been bombarded with these types of calls and I have done what many other people have done. Out of frustration I have:

- Hung up on them.
- Asked them to hang on and then walked away.
- Politely refused their goods or service.
- Been aggressive back to aggressive callers.
- Played music to them.
- Asked them annoying questions.
- Sworn at them.
- Let the answer phone screen my calls.
- Used the anonymous call barring service my telephone company provides.
- Pretend I don't speak English.
- Talk back with utter nonsense.

However, none of these tactics worked and in some cases, only made it worse. I kept asking myself why on earth a company would keep calling back when I had made it clear that I really did not want their product or service.

I asked a former call centre worker why telesales people keep calling consumers who argue with them and he sheepishly told me that sometimes, they just do it to wind up people who seem to be easily wound, regardless of the fact they are breaking the law.

Some call centres seem to have a high staff turn over, so the last person who called you may have left the company without making a note of the fact that you said you did not want to be contacted again.

So the list with your number on gets passed to a new worker who calls you yet again.

If the list of tactics I have used in the past does not seem to work, is there anything that can be done? The answer is yes, there most certainly is. However, it requires you to be pro-active and take up some of your own time to take the appropriate action, but the results are worth it.

You will need to familiarise yourself with what UK law says about Direct Marketing because that is your main weapon in the war against unwanted communications.

You need to understand all the different types of Direct Marketing communications and what the law says about each one.

As the laws can be a little confusing for some people, I have pulled together the information you will need to launch an effective campaign to protect your privacy and peace at home as far as possible.

Chapter 2 - What are the laws that deal with Direct Marketing activities?

First of all, you should know there are three things designed to protect us from the negative side of Direct Marketing. They are:

- Specific legislation designed to ensure Direct Marketing is carried out according to strict rules.
- Official guidelines explaining to companies how to carry out their Direct Marketing activities legally.
- Organisations set up to monitor the activities of those who ignore the law and take action against persistent offenders.

In other words, there are laws against harassing consumers with unwanted Direct Marketing activities and there are organisations there to enforce the law when people choose to ignore it. However, those organisations need to know it is happening and who is doing it. This is where you, as a victim, are required to take action.

The main UK laws and regulations relevant to Direct Marketing are:

- **The Data Protection Act 1998 (the DPA)**
- **The Privacy and Electronic Communications (EC Directive) Regulations 2003 (the PECR)**
- **The Communications Act 2003**

The organisations responsible for regulating these laws are:

- **The Information Commissioner's Office (the ICO)**
- **OfCom**

In law, these organisations have huge powers when it comes to how your personal data is processed and used. When companies call your telephone or send you e-mails and texts, they are using your personal data and are therefore subject to abiding by the very strict laws that state what they can and cannot do with all the methods of contacting you.

One of the factors involved in the rise of nuisance calls, texts, emails and junk-mail seems to be that many people are not aware of the very robust laws governing Direct Marketing and they simply put up with the constant intrusions into their daily lives instead of taking positive action to stop it. In taking positive action, you can help stop the erosion of your right to be left in peace in your own home.

There are also other regulatory bodies with rules and codes of industry practice. For example, there is the **Direct Marketing Association** that publishes the **Direct Marketing Code of Practice**. However, for our purposes, as consumers, we need only to concentrate on the laws and regulations I have listed and, on the bodies that regulate them.

Chapter 3 - What are the ICO and OfCom?

The Information Commissioner's Office is 'the UK's independent authority set up to uphold information rights in the public interest promoting openness by public bodies and data privacy for individuals.'

But what does that actually mean? In simple terms, it means they are there to help protect our personal information (also called data) from misuse. Our personal details are very valuable to online criminals and legitimate businesses alike. In 2012, the Metropolitan Police warned that identity theft could begin with a criminal knowing only three pieces of your personal information. However, many of us freely give our personal details away online everyday without even thinking about how they will be used.

The ICO is the body that helps to protect, in law, how our information is stored and used. The ICO is also there to educate us on the responsibilities we have to protect our own information. The ICO also regulates the Data Protection Act 1998 and the Privacy and Electronic Communications (EC Directive) Regulations 2003.

If the unwanted communications we are receiving are in breach of either law, the ICO is the body we should turn to for help. The ICO takes breaches very seriously and is active in pursuing those who persistently offend.

The ICO needs us to report persistent nuisance communications so they can take the appropriate action against those who flout the law. This applies to live calls, recorded messages, texts, emails, and fax messages.

Note – The ICO does not cover silent calls. Silent calls come under the remit of OfCom

---

OfCom

This is the communications regulator in the UK. It regulates landline and mobile phones, the TV and radio sectors, postal services and the airwaves over which wireless devices operate.

OfCom makes sure that people in the UK get the best from their communications services and are protected from undesirable practices, while ensuring that competition can thrive.

Ofcom operates under a number of Acts of Parliament, including, in particular, the Communications Act 2003. Ofcom must act within the powers and duties set for it by Parliament in legislation.

The laws and regulations that the ICO and OfCom oversee are outlined below.

The Data Protection Act 1998 (DPA)

The DPA is based around eight principles of how data should be handled. When companies or organisations contact us to try and sell goods or services, they are using our personal data to do so.

The Act's definition of personal data is any information that can be used to identify a living individual. That includes your name, address, telephone number or email address. The DPA covers information stored on, or intended to be stored on, a computer or held in a 'relevant filing system'. A relevant filing system could even mean a notebook used by a sales person if it contains lists of names and numbers to call.

The Privacy and Electronic Communications (EC Directive) Regulations 2003 (PECR)

The PECR provides rules about sending unsolicited marketing and advertising by electronic means such as by telephone, fax, email, text and picture or video message or by using an automated calling system. The PECR also includes other rules relating to cookies (pieces of information left on your computer by websites), telephone directories, traffic data, location data and security breaches.

The DPA and the PECR together provide you with substantial protection from unwanted communications in any form. The key is knowing how they protect you and what you can do to use their power when people invade your privacy with unwanted phone-calls and messages.

How your personal data is used is taken very seriously by the ICO which enforces both the Data Protection Act and the Privacy and Electronic Communications (EC Directive) Regulations 2003

The Communications Act 2003

This Act is a wide-ranging and complicated piece of legislation. For our purposes, all we really need to know is it covers the improper use of a public electronic communications network which includes making silent or abandoned calls. It is OfCom that enforces this act.

Chapter 4 - So what is 'Direct Marketing'?

According to section 11 of the Data Protection Act 1998, Direct Marketing is:

'the communication (by whatever means) of any advertising or marketing material which is directed to particular individuals.'

There are two kinds of Direct Marketing:

- Solicited - or in other words, marketing you have asked for in some way.
- Unsolicited - marketing you have definitely not asked for.

The DPA and the PECR both limit the way businesses and organisations can carry out Direct Marketing that a consumer has not asked for.

In the eyes of the ICO, Direct Marketing does not just mean anything that is being sold. They regard Direct Marketing as:

" a wide range of activities that applies not just to the offer for sale of goods and services, but also to the promotion of an organisation's aims and ideals."

They clearly state that this includes charities and political parties.

Therefore Direct Marketing does not just mean selling, it means things like surveys and other activities designed to get information from you or to promote something.

Chapter 5 - Are nuisance Direct Marketing calls just happening to you?

No - definitely not. Sometimes, particularly with nuisance phone calls where the caller's number is blocked, it can feel personal.

Some sections of the population, particularly the elderly or vulnerable, can feel under personal attack when they receive a stream of marketing calls they do not want or understand. Silent calls are especially frightening to some people. It can raise suspicions about the true nature of such calls and make people feel intimidated. It can make elderly people living alone feel fearful about answering the phone.

One couple in their 80s talked to us about their recent experiences with marketing calls and what they told us made it very clear that there are many companies out there who are still prepared to break the law in order to try and sell products or services.

At the time of writing this book, the couple was regularly receiving a mix of live calls, recordings and silent calls, all of which caused them great anxiety. This reaction is not uncommon and is precisely why we need laws controlling the actions of business owners and organisations that would otherwise not consider the negative effects of their invasive marketing activities.

However, it isn't just the elderly whose sense of well-being can be affected by marketing calls. Not everyone will feel anxious after receiving such calls but they can cause people to feel stressed and annoyed if they are frequent and persistent.

One person we spoke to told us that she felt unwanted sales calls coming into her home were like shop owners dragging her into their shops and forcing her to look at their goods when she was simply walking past with no intention of buying anything. She told us that each time she has to deal with another call, she feels her right to peace and privacy at home is being violated. When these violations occur over and over again, they can cause people to feel angry, resentful and in some cases intimidated.

Unfortunately for those of us who do not want such intrusions into our homes, the business world now sees us as 'prospects' rather than people with rights and refers to us as such. Some sales callers do not see us human beings being bothered in our own homes; to them, we are nothing more than the prospect of a sum of money.

In some cases, our reaction will determine how big their wage packet is and possibly how long they keep their job. Given this, some unprofessional callers are going to be aggressive in their attitude if you do not react in the way they hoped you would. However, their job security or income is not your problem. You have the right, in law, not to be victimised through your landline telephone, mobile phone or computer.

Chapter 6 - What kind of nuisance calls are people getting?

There are several types of invasive advertising methods currently being used by businesses and organisations to target 'prospects' in their own homes. It is known in the business world as 'Direct Marketing' and can come through your landline, mobile phone, computer, tablet or your front door in the form of junk mail (an issue not covered in this book). The methods causing the most concern for consumers at the moment and which are covered in this book are:

- Phone calls made by real live people
- Phone calls made by an automated system that plays a recording to you
- Silent phone calls
- Texts to mobile phones
- E-mails

All of these types of contact can be disturbing for people who don't want them and can, in some cases, turn the telephone into an enemy if the calls are persistent.

In recent years, many people have been getting calls from people trying to sell them solar panels, insulation, double glazing or boiler replacements. Many people have also been getting calls about claiming money back for various things such as accidents or mis-sold payment protection insurance (PPI).

The reason for the calls about solar panels and boiler replacement is most likely because in the last few years, the government has been offering various incentives to consumers for making their homes more energy efficient.

One such incentive for consumers was launched in June 2014 when a government backed private company had a pot of money worth £120 million to pay out in the form of loans for energy saving measures such as:

- Loft insulation.
- Wall insulation.
- Roof insulation.
- Hot water tank insulation.
- Draught proofing.
- Boiler replacement etc.

In order to qualify for a loan, you had to prove that the savings made by the energy saving measure would cover the cost of the loan. So the company had an army of approved assessors ready to assess homes for energy saving potential and to calculate whether the savings made would justify a loan.

There were also approved installers ready to install the insulation, boiler or draught proofing you had obtained a loan for. All they needed were the customers that stood in between them and their share of the £120 million pot of money.

It was in the best interests of 'green energy' installers to convince as many people as possible to be assessed for home improvements in order to get their hands on as much of the pot of cash as possible. This goes some way to explaining why the nation was bombarded with persistent calls about boiler replacement etc.

In the run up to when the new green energy deal was launched in June 2014, there was a massive increase in the number of concerns about sales calls reported to the Information Commissioner's Office (ICO), the independent UK body set up to uphold our information rights and protect our data privacy. They said:

"The number of concerns reported about sales calls, including live and automated calls, has increased over the first three months of the financial year, from 11,276 in April 2014, 13,500 in May to 15,890 in June. Concerns reported about calls are at their highest levels since April 2013."

That is an increase of 4,614 calls in only three months. Many of the calls were, according to the ICO, about boilers, insulation and solar panels. They say that between April 2014 and June 2014, they received just under 9,000 concerns relating to unwanted automated sales calls about boilers alone.

Remember, those 9,000 concerns were reported by people that actually contacted the ICO; there is no way of knowing how many more than that were harassed but did not know they could reach out and tell someone in authority.

Chapter 7 - What usually happens during the different types of calls?

Live Calls

Live calls often begin with a bright and breezy voice asking if you are the homeowner. They may or may not know your name, depending on how they got your phone number. Whether they know your name or not is significant because it plays a part in which law governs what they are doing.

Some callers will say your name and ask if you are that person. They may try and engage you in friendly chit chat to gain your confidence and they may tell you their company name which often has the words 'green' or 'energy' in it somewhere.

Live callers will often start their spiel with the phrase "don't worry, I'm not selling anything!" before going on to inform you about a service or ask you questions to gain deeper information about you.

> **Tip – Remember, even if they are 'not selling anything' – the law still applies and the caller cannot justify calling you just because they are 'not selling anything'.**

The caller may only have your number with no other details such as name, address, age, sex, status etc and may be trying to gather more information for a database. They may also be criminals trying to get your bank account details.

These callers are often highly trained to keep you from hanging up and, to get something out of the call. You can be absolutely confident that no business is spending hard cash employing people to call you up for a friendly chat! Do not be fooled; the aim of the call will be to gain something from you in the form of a sale or further personal information about members of the household.

Some people who are particularly vulnerable to these types of calls are those who are housebound, living alone and who do not speak to many people each day. A seemingly friendly caller can bring some much needed human contact into the life of a person who is lonely. If you are such a person, be extra careful of who you let into your home via the telephone, it can be just as dangerous as letting someone in through your front door.

Always remember, no matter what the caller says or how friendly they may be, they have a job to do and that job involves getting money or valuable information from you.

If you are reading this and happen to be someone who is elderly and lonely, you can call **Age UK** Advice: 0800 169 6565 to find out about befriending services in your area. If you are online you can contact Age UK via their website

www.ageuk.org.uk/health-wellbeing/relationships-and-family/befriending-services-combating-loneliness/

Calls made by an automated system that plays a recording

Typically, when you answer the phone to this type of call, you hear a recorded announcement that may be something like, 'you are entitled to a free boiler replacement'. Or, it may be about getting debt wiped out. The message will then invite you to press a number on your phone to be put through to a live sales person.

These recorded messages often make statements that cannot be relied on to be true. In the case of boiler replacements for example, while there may be people who are eligible for grants, you may not be one of them. Remember, the company calling may not be interested in whether you can get a grant or not, they may simply want money regardless of whether it comes from a grant or from your bank account. I received dozens of these calls before they drove me to take action to stop them and we are definitely not eligible for a free boiler replacement - however, the calls we received told us we were.

They say this, it seems, to entice us to go through to a live sales person where you may discover that you are not entitled to a free boiler replacement after all but, not to worry (they say), you can get a loan! (Note - the government backed deal was closed for loans at the end of July 2014 as the entire £120 million pot had been used up). However, this may change in the future if the government launches any similar schemes.

Consumers have also been bombarded with recorded calls urging them to claim compensation for accidents they never had. The companies making these calls are hoping that if they call enough people, they will, by the law of averages, hit on people who really did have accidents and who they can then encourage to make compensation claims which the callers cash in on in various ways.

Silent calls

These kinds of calls are by far the most disturbing of all, particularly to the elderly and other potentially vulnerable people. They are exactly what the label says - silent. The phone rings but when you answer, there is no one there.

A machine called a 'predictive dialler', also known as a 'bulk dialler', makes the vast majority of these calls. The machines are used by call centres to call large numbers of people at the same time. As soon as the call is answered by you at home, the machine should then connect you to a real person in the call centre. Unfortunately, the machines often generate more calls than can be handled by call centre staff. This results in the call being 'dropped' or abandoned because when you pick up at home, all the call handlers are busy with other calls. This results in a silent call for those on the other end.

These types of calls were very common before 2006 when the

nation was bombarded with silent and abandoned calls from bulk diallers. Since 2006 action has been taken by OfCom, the independent regulator for UK communications industries and, by the government to prevent this type of harassment of consumers at home. However, silent calls are still a problem because of unscrupulous companies who choose to ignore the legislation designed to stop them.

Unwanted texts, e-mails and picture or video messages.

These types of communications are all classed by the PECR as electronic mail. Problems can occur when you are receiving numerous unwanted messages and e-mails that overshadow the messages from friends and family. Many people these days complain of having to delete a large amount of electronic 'junk mail' from their computers, phones, laptops and tablets.

Chapter 8 - So what can I do to stop all this?

First, know the law. The Data Protection Act 1998 (DPA) and the Privacy and Electronic Communications (EC Directive) Regulations 2003 (PECR) both restrict the way organisations can carry out Direct Marketing that has not specifically been asked for by the consumer (unsolicited marketing material).

If a company is using any of the following methods to contact people, they must always comply with the PECR:

- Telephone
- Automated calling system
- E Mail
- Fax
- Text
- Picture or video message

If the company knows the name of the person they are contacting, they must also comply with the DPA.

Therefore if a company calls you from a list of numbers but does not know your name, the DPA does not apply, however, as soon as they know your name, it does apply.

If you receive a Direct Marketing call and the caller addresses you by your name then you know immediately there are two pieces of legislation covering the Direct Marketing activities of the company.

If you receive a Direct Marketing call where the caller clearly has no idea who you are, then you know there is one piece of legislation covering their activities. Once they know your name, you are covered by both pieces of legislation.

Chapter 9 - So what do the DPA 1998, PECR and the Communications Act 2003 say about Direct Marketing?

There are different rules for different types of communications and at a quick glance, even the simplified versions of the rules can seem unclear. The problem, for the average person, of working out whether a company may or may not contact you is caused by the confusion around the obtaining of your consent.

Certain types of communications, such as emails, texts, faxes, picture messages and video for example, can only be used for unsolicited Direct Marketing if a company has your consent to do so – which seems clear enough. However, when you begin to look at what the PECR says about consent and what that actually is, it all gets a little confusing. Here is an outline of what the law seems to say about each method of communication.

Live calls

The type of calls where a real live person calls you come under the rules of the PECR and, if they know your name, under the rules of the DPA as well.

Under the law, it appears that organisations can make unsolicited sales calls to you BUT they are obligated to first check your number against the Telephone Preference Service to see if you have opted out (more about that on page 30).

In that case, they especially need to comply with the first principle of the DPA. This means they can only make marketing calls to you if it is 'fair to do so'.

This means they must have obtained your contact details fairly and lawfully and that you are aware the organisation has your number and is planning to use it for marketing purposes.

The company must not make any calls that a person would not reasonably expect or which would cause them 'unjustified harm'.

An example of calling somebody unfairly would be if their contact details were obtained from a third party list and the company didn't check to see if the person had agreed to their details being passed on; there are strict rules regarding the buying and selling of marketing lists.

Once a person has told a caller that they do not want any further sales calls, the company must stop calling.

According to the law, even if you are registered with the TPS, a company may still call you IF you have given your consent. The giving of consent seems to be a grey area open to interpretation and may be why so many companies are breaking the rules.

Automated calls (where a recording speaks to you, instead of a live person)

These types of calls, where you answer the phone to find a recorded message being played, also come under the PECR rules, which are stricter than with live calls. This is because recorded calls are considered to be particularly intrusive and unsettling for people to receive. The law, therefore, takes a firm stance when it comes to the use of automated calls for Direct Marketing.

Once again, under the law, a company may only make such calls if it has the consent of the person being called. The company is also required to include their identity in the call along with a contact address or free-phone number so you can easily opt out of future calls.

Even if you are NOT registered with the TPS, the company is still not allowed to call you unless they have your permission to make automated, recorded calls to you. With live calls they can contact you if you are not registered but with recorded calls, they must not.

Silent calls

These are the types of calls generated by bulk diallers and are perhaps the most frightening of all nuisance Direct Marketing calls. In 2006, OfCom introduced some very strict rules to tackle the issue of silent calls and fined a number of big companies for infringing them.

At the time, the maximum fine was £50,000 however, that figure has now risen to £2 million so there are some very good reasons why Direct Marketers need to sit up and take note.

It is now against the law for a company to make a call that results in silence when you answer it. OfCom says that no more than 3% of all calls made by a bulk-dialler can result in being abandoned and even those ones must not be silent.

They must play a brief information message to let the person who has received the call know what it was about.

The company must make sure their number is visible and they must not call again within 72 hours.

Remember - ALL automated calls need the consent of the person being called.

E Mails, Text, Fax and picture or video messages.

These methods of contact all require the consent of the person being contacted before a company can send them any communications.

Chapter 10 - Actions To Take to Minimise Nuisance Direct Marketing

Now that you have a brief insight into the laws that protect you and the organisations that enforce them, you are ready to take some action.

Your first port of call is the Telephone Preference Service.

The Telephone Preference Service (TPS)

This service is designed to protect you from unsolicited sales calls. It is a statutory list of numbers that anyone can register their landline and/or mobile phone number with to prevent Direct Marketing phone calls. The legislation associated with the TPS is the PECR.

If you haven't already done so, you will need to register with the TPS. You can do this online at www.tpsonline.org . Or, you can call them on 0845 070 0707 to register your number. Alternatively, you can write to the TPS at:

Telephone Preference Service (TPS)

DMA House

70 Margaret Street

London

W1W 8SS

Or e-mail at tps@dma.org.uk

Once you have done this, you have officially opted out of receiving Direct Marketing calls. You can register any live number including landline and mobile numbers. It can take up to 28 days for your registration to be effective but after that, being registered SHOULD protect you from unwanted marketing calls. During this

28 day period, a company can still call you UNLESS you have specifically told them you do not want them to call any more, in which case, they should usually cease straight away.

Of course, as you may have found if you are already registered with the TPS, this does not mean you will definitely stop getting all sales calls.

But what it does mean is that you are in a stronger position to challenge the callers and to do this you need to be friendly towards the caller rather than hostile. I will explain.

I have been registered with the TPS for several years but it did not stop the spate of Direct Marketing calls I have received in the past three years. When they began, I dealt with them badly because I had no knowledge of the law and as a result, the employees of one particular company began to call daily on my landline.

The calls went on for two years and when I blocked them by barring anonymous callers to my landline, two individuals took to calling me on my landline and mobile phone from various mobile numbers. When I familiarised myself with the law and the kind of fines that were being handed out to big companies for persistently harassing people, I changed my whole approach.

The main thing to do is to be warm and friendly to the caller, even if you are annoyed at being disturbed yet again. The reason for being friendly is to gain the caller's confidence enough for them to drop their guard and reveal who they are. It is very hard for the TPS, ICO or OfCom to do anything about callers whose identity and contact details you do not know.

The law requires Direct Marketers to make their contact details clearly known and they must provide you with a way of opting out of future calls. However, many callers withhold their number or display a fake one and do not tell you who they are. So your main aim is to find that out. The only way I have found to do that is to be ultra-friendly and give the impression I might be interested in what they have to say.

Be VERY careful however NOT to give away any more details about yourself or confirm any that they are not sure of, such as confirming your name. Be 'warm' but protect yourself – guard your personal information as if it is the key to your bank account.

Your aim is to find out more about THEM not for them to find out more about YOU.

Engage in the chit chat they offer and sound interested without agreeing to anything. Then, when you have established some rapport, ask who they are; get a company name and contact details, the more the better and try, if you can, to check them out online as you are talking. Ask them in a friendly way, where they got your number and make a note of anything they say. If it isn't clear, push the issue – but maintain the warmth in your voice.

Once you are happy that you now know the company contact details and that you would have something to provide in a complaint to the ICO, you can become more formal and challenge the caller. However, be assertive rather than aggressive or they will probably hang up before you have stated your case.

You begin the formal part of the conversation by telling the caller you are registered with the TPS and ask why the company is not complying with the law by screening numbers against the TPS list.

When I began to do this, I had call centre workers tell me it wasn't their job to do that. I had all sorts of reactions but I remained calm and friendly and asked them to please pass information up the chain of command to the top, to let managers know the company was breaking the law by calling my number.

At this point, you formally request they cease calling and state that you will be passing their details to the TPS as a company that is not screening against the TPS lists. Then explain you will be logging any future calls and passing the record on to the ICO in the form of a complaint.

If the caller is still on the line by this point – and many of them will be - ask if they are aware of the massive fines being handed out to companies who ignore the law. Then say clearly, "I want you to ensure my number is suppressed and not available for use anymore". (This is important because if they just delete your number, there is no record that says this is a number to avoid and it may come up again from another list in the future.)

What I found, after taking this approach with every caller, was that most calls stopped immediately. Being aggressive with nuisance callers just doesn't work and can actually make them worse.

I still get the odd automated call where I am asked to press a number to speak to an operator and on one occasion, I did press to be put through. I then did my 'friendly' act until I had the company details. I then asked them if they believed they had my consent to make automated calls to me and was met with a load of defensive nonsense.

I calmly stated that the law says they need the person's consent to make automated calls and that I would be reporting them to the ICO about this and any future calls. I then mentioned the hefty fines, which can run into hundreds of thousands of pounds and in the case of silent calls, up to £2 million.

In the case of automated calls, even if you are not registered with the TPS, companies still should not bother you with pre-recorded messages because they need your specific permission to make such calls, regardless of whether you are TPS registered or not.

The methods I have described here for tackling nuisance Direct Marketing calls will not stop persistent callers who flout the law.

For some companies, even the heftiest fines are nothing more than an annoyance compared to what they make out of their Direct Marketing activities - however, I have found it does deter most of the nuisance callers.

Since I took this approach, I have hardly been bothered by Direct Marketing calls.

It is worth noting here that at the time of writing this book, many people were receiving nuisance calls from companies and individuals actively breaking the law by concealing their identities and continuing to call people even when asked to stop.

My research showed me that such callers are staying one step ahead of the enforcement bodies who are continually trying to combat the problem.

Unfortunately, it seems that there are some nuisance calls that we can do nothing to stop at this moment in time. There are gadgets on the market that claim to prevent all nuisance calls and some have very good reviews but it appears they cannot prevent ALL nuisance calls.

I cannot recommend any particular gadget but for those online, if you Google 'nuisance call blocker' you will see for yourself what is available. Amazon is a good starting point and the customer reviews give a good idea of what is working well for people who have tried various call blockers. One machine called TrueCall – The Nuisance Call Blocker has 289 reviews and 236 of those are 5 star so it may be worth considering but as I said, I cannot recommend it as I have not tried any call blocking gadgets myself.

Chapter 11 - A Word of Caution About Recorded Calls

Although I have mentioned an instance where I responded to an automated call by pressing a number to be put through to a live agent, I would not necessarily recommend doing this. As I have said, at the time of writing this, there seemed to be an outbreak of recorded calls instigated by people who appear to be ignoring the law. They are withholding their caller ID and do not identify themselves in the recorded message. Nor do they leave any contact details for you to call to opt out of future calls.

Many people have told me they have received such calls and my belief is that their evasion of the law is deliberate rather than out of ignorance. A friend of mine had one such call about replacement boilers recently and when she pressed to be put through to a live agent to tell them to stop calling, she got another recording saying they were all busy but would call back.

A man did call her back but when my friend said her piece and pointed out he did not have her consent to call, he said he did because she had pressed 2 to be put through!

When she explained that she only did this to be able to speak to a live person to stop the calls, he insisted he could now ring whenever he wanted. She is now being plagued with recorded calls daily by this company who are using several different numbers.

My friend is now reporting each number as the calls happen, to the ICO on their special online form.

Chapter 12 - What To Do About Unsolicited emails, Texts and Picture messages

As stated earlier, the law says that Direct Marketers need your consent before they can send you any form of electronic marketing material. However, I have found the whole area around consent to be confusing.

People who regularly use the internet to buy goods and services can, if they are not careful, become victims of unclear policies and may unwittingly give their consent for Direct Marketing material to be sent even though the law says they must make their intentions clear.

The rules about what constitutes consent can seem confusing. Rules about opt outs, opt ins and soft opt ins can tie your brain up in knots.

Sometime last year, I signed up with a website to do 'paid surveys'. That was a big mistake. Within a very short time, I began to receive all sorts of marketing e-mails from people I had never heard of. After almost a year of this, I got fed up and began to call the companies (one was a well known national gym) and ask where they got my email address.

I was astounded as I went through a chain of four organisations and finally arrived at the culprit company who seemed absolutely affronted that I had called to challenge them. A very disgruntled but well spoken woman informed me that it was most unusual to be called up and asked these sorts of questions.

I did say, welcome to my world, I am sick of it too! I explained that they had passed my details on to a company that had then passed them on three more times and that I was getting e-mail advertising I did not want. I asked how they had obtained my contact details and why they were passing them around like sweets.

Eventually, after 14 days of pushing and waiting, I had an e-mail from another part of the company explaining that when I signed up to do surveys, I agreed to receive marketing material.

The e-mail said it would have been very clear what I was signing up for at the time - however, I doubt it was or I would not have signed up. She told me that to opt out now, I would have to contact all the advertisers myself by ticking opt out boxes at the end of each email.

However after I made a huge fuss and demanded that THEY stop it all, I didn't get any further advertising.

The point is, the law is there if you want to go to the trouble of contacting these people and then challenge them. Most legitimate companies will listen when they realise you mean business and that you will complain to the ICO if they do not stop.

I believe the reaction of the woman when I rang up to ask what on earth they were doing passing my details around says it all – she said it was 'most unusual to be challenged in that way'. Perhaps we are all too accepting of this growing nuisance and not waving the laws and rules that should protect us, in their faces hard enough.

So if you are being bombarded with unwanted junk electronic mail, I suggest you invest some time in contacting a few of the companies to officially tell them to stop and ask where they got your details in the first place.

I found it was a waste of time trying to work out whether I had or had not given consent. So I decided that as yesterday has gone, it was time to move on and start afresh with each junk e-mail.

You can do this too. Start by scrolling down to the bottom of any marketing emails or texts you are getting and click on unsubscribe. Direct Marketers are required by law to provide you with an easy way to opt out of future communications. If you are getting e-mails and texts from companies who are not giving you an easy way to opt out then you need to report them to the ICO. Just keep on doing this and you should see your junk e-mails and texts greatly diminish.

Since I started getting more vocal and assertive, all the Direct Marketing I was getting in various forms has greatly lessened.

Use the ICO website to report persistent offenders and start being VERY careful about accidentally opting in to receiving Direct Marketing material that you do not actually want.

We need to start being much more protective of our contact details because they are worth a lot of money to the people who want to get at us in our own homes. It would be great to get back to the days when business owners sat in their shops waiting for us to show up when we actually want something. Now, they are there day and night, hammering away at us through our home telephones, computers, mobile phones and tablets trying to psych us into parting with our cash.

There will always be a criminal element in this world that will flout the law no matter what. Whilst we cannot stop every nuisance caller, texter or e-mailer, we can stop most of them.

Be strong! Fight back! The law is there, use it.

Chapter 13 - Further information

For further information, you can visit these websites:

www.tpsonline.org.uk (See phone number and mailing address on page 29)

www.ico.org.uk

Head Office
Information Commissioner's Office
Wycliffe House
Water Lane
Wilmslow
Cheshire
SK9 5AF

Tel: 0303 123 1113 (local rate) or 01625 545 745 if you prefer to use a national rate number

Fax: 01625 524 510

www.ofcom.org.uk/

Ofcom
Riverside House
2a Southwark Bridge Road
London SE1 9HA
If you want advice or to complain to Ofcom please call them on 0300 123 3333 or 020 7981 3040. They are open Monday to Friday from 9.00am to 5.00pm.

The information provided in this book does not constitute legal advice and should not be used as such. This book is for information purposes only and whilst every effort has been made to ensure the information was correct at the time of writing, we cannot guarantee there are no errors.

If you have a legal issue with Direct Marketing activities, we suggest you contact the ICO or a solicitor for advice.

www.ingramcontent.com/pod-product-compliance
Lightning Source LLC
Chambersburg PA
CBHW070510290526
45790CB00003B/1181